Green Is The Thing!!!

Money Management
For Kids:

$ $ $

By: Tyrik Wynn &
T. Wynn

D0169808

ISBN: 1511771097
ISBN-13: 978-1511771092

$ Introduction $

Years ago, when I was around eight years old, I noticed that my mom (T. Wynn) would go to this same place every week. So, one day I asked her.

"Mom, what is this place called?"

"This is a bank."

"What do you do at the bank?"

"The bank is a place that keeps our money safe. We have this thing called an account, and that is where we put our money."

"Why do they have to keep your money?"

"This is a way for us to save money, and when we need some of our money, we can come and get it out."

"Wow that sounds cool! Can I open an account?"

"Yes, your dad and I will bring you back next week, so you can open your own savings account."

"Cool, thanks mom."

This is how managing my money started for me. My parents explained to me the importance of saving your money, and to be careful how you spend it. In this book, I will outline the different ways that kids can learn to make, save, and manage their green (money).

Table Of Contents

Chapter 1
$ Making the Green $

As a kid, we often think that we can't get jobs. So, what can we do to earn money? Some of the ways that many of us receive money is from our birthdays, Christmas gift, weekly allowances from doing chores, and even sometimes for getting good grades. There are some other creative ways that we can earn money also.

Did you know that there are some kids that actually own their own business? They are called entrepreneurs. You can become an entrepreneur also by starting a business by doing several different things.

These are just a few examples. You could start a lawn business, where you go around your neighborhood and rake leaves, or clean the trash out of people yards. When you get a little older you could learn to cut grass, and add that to your lawn business. Washing cars and helping your neighbors clean out their garages is another bright idea.

One business you can do that will help you make money, and help with the environment is to start a recycling business. Collecting cans, plastic bottles, and newspapers in your neighborhood, then taking them to a recycling bin can earn you money. You will need your parents help with this, because they will have to take you to the recycling place.

Some kids even have businesses that they run over the internet, by selling old items that they no longer use.
Or, they will ask their parents to help them with a yard sale and sell some of their items.

If there are people with dogs in your community, you could start a dog walking business. On trash day, you can take each neighbor's trash can to the curb for pick up, and return it once the trash truck has picked it up, because many people forget to do this each week. You can keep a list of all the people that you do this for. These people will be called your customers.

To get customers, you can make a

flyer on the computer and pass them out to your neighbors. Be careful when doing this, and have an adult with you when you approach someone's home. Remember to look presentable when you approach potential customers. You do not have to wear a suit, but always have on clean clothes, your shirt tucked in, and your pants pulled up. Also, make sure you speak loud and clear, and use correct language when talking to your future customers, and explain your business to them in detail, look them in the eyes, and give a firm hand shake at the end.

Once you start your business, you must be serious about it. You will have to stay on top of it so it can be successful. If you think you will not have the time to dedicate to the business, then do not start one. It will not look good if you start a business and not be able to handle the task of doing it. Write down exactly what you are doing in your business, and what items and supplies you will need for the business. Decide if you will be able to run the business yourself, or will you need your friends or parents to help, and what times you will be able to run the business. You must also see how much money it will cost you to start your business. Do research on the internet about the business so you will know exactly what it will take to run this business.

Make sure you are always on time for your customers, if you tell them you will be there between certain time periods and then make sure you are there. If any emergencies come up which will cause you to not be there, then make sure the customers are contacted to know you will not be there that day. When you start a business, it is supposed to grow and expand, but it will not do that if you do not treat your customers right and with respect.

So, as you can see there are several different things that you can do as a kid to earn money. Before you start any business, always talk with your parents or guardians to make sure that they approve of what you are doing. They may even give you other ideas for a business.

Remember, that one day this small kid business could turn into a million-dollar company that you could be running as an adult. So, take it serious, but make sure it is something that you will enjoy doing.

Chapter 2
$ Saving Your Green $

In my introduction, I talked about putting money in a bank and saving it. All kids can open a savings account. You just have to have your parents or guardian's permission, and they have to go to the bank with you.

A savings account is an account where you put money in, and the bank keeps it for you until you want to take it out, but try to avoid taking money out which is called a withdrawal, unless it is for an emergency. Once you open your savings account, remember to keep up with how much money you put in it, which is called a deposit. Keep a record of all your deposits and withdrawals, so you will know how much money you have in the bank, which is called your balance.

Having your money in a savings account can help you make more money. There is this thing called interest, where the bank pays you, for letting them keep your money. The interest amount can vary, and the people at the bank can tell you what amount your money will earn.

There is another item that you can get to help save your money. It is called a savings bond. Savings bonds are issued by the U.S government. Your parents or anyone else who wants to help you save money can buy these for you. To get them, they will have to go online to www.TreasuryDirect.gov to order them for you. They are like money, but you can't take it to a store or anything like that, you have to take them to the bank and exchange them for cash. They can be bought in different amounts from $25 to $10,000.

This is a great way to save money for college, if they are purchased at a young age. When you have savings bonds, and keep them for years, then you earn interest, which means it will be worth more than the amount that is printed on the savings bond. You and your parents can read more about them on the website listed above.

Some banks offer an account that you

can use just for saving money for Christmas, it is called The Christmas Club. The account is created so that you or other people can put money in the account throughout the year, and when it comes time to shop for Christmas gifts, you can withdraw the money. This account is different from your regular savings account, because remember with a savings account, you will try not to take money out of it to spend.

This here is a way for your parents to save money for you. It's called Upromise, this is an account that puts money towards your college fund. If your parents sign up for it at www.upromise.com, they can earn money from purchases that they make at different businesses, and it goes into an account that helps pay for college.

There are several other ways to save money, including getting a mutual fund which involves dealing with the stock market. Your parents could look up information on this, and talk to someone who is a financial advisor, that can help them set up many of these different saving funds for you. If you are not able to get any of these savings accounts right now, then you could always put your money in your piggy bank, or make your own money jars. Remember, you are never too young to start saving your money, so talk with your parents or guardians today about these savings ideas.

You may not know the meaning of the some of the words that I used in this chapter, but don't worry. I put a glossary in the back of the book, which explains them.

Chapter 3
$ Spending Your Green Wisely $

As kids we always see toys, video games, clothes, and shoes that we want. We really don't realize the value of money, and think that our parents should be able to buy everything that we want. Once you start making your own money, you will realize the value of a dollar, and will learn to spend it wisely.

My parents taught me a lesson once when it came to spending my money. Whenever we would go out to eat, I would always want to go to places that cost a lot, or if we went to a fast food restaurant, I would never want anything off the dollar menu.

One day my dad gave me $10. It was my pay from when I helped him at his business. We went to a restaurant, and my dad said that I had to pay for my own food. Well, I did not want to spend all of my money, but I wanted a combo that cost about $6. I ended up ordering from the dollar menu that day and only spent $3. I finally realized that it does cost a lot for all of us to eat out. Then I started adding up how much my parents probably spend on food when we go out, and it is a lot.

Once I saw what it was like to spend my own money, I began to value it more and my parent's money more. You always need to be careful about how you spend your money, because you don't want to spend it all up and be broke. Once the money is spent on food or toys you cannot get it back.

When you do spend your money, and buy something from a store. You need to make sure you can count money correctly, so you will have enough to buy your items, and to also make sure you get the correct change back. Sometimes people may make a mistake and not give you enough money back, or give you too much money back. You need to watch out for these types of mistakes. If you are not given enough money back, which is called your change, then let the person know. If they give you too much money back, you need to be honest and let them know about this also.

It is ok to buy some things that you want, but always save more than what you spend. If you practice this while you are young, then it will help you when you become an adult. You must know how to manage money, in order to live well as an adult.

Chapter 4
$ Be Giving with Your Green $

I have always been taught by my parents, that you should be a giving person. No, this does not mean that you should give all your money or things away, but it is good to help out people when they truly need it.

My family and I go to church regularly and we are Christians. When I go to church, I pay my tithes and offerings. Tithes and offerings are when you give money to the church, to show honor to God. It shows respect and thanks to God for all the blessings that He has given you.

Showing honor to God does not always involve money, you can be a blessing to people by volunteering at different charities, or offering to help other people out without charging them. I am a part of an after-school program and we volunteered at different places throughout the city. There are several places in need of volunteers no matter what city you live in. You should always try to make a difference in your community. You can even make it a family event and all of you can go and volunteer together. It will make you feel good to give back to others.

Try to also give back to your parents, because they have done so much for you. I sometimes offer to buy my parents dinner and give them gifts on special occasions, and I use my own money to do it. It makes me feel good to do things for them and other family members.

$ Conclusion $

I hope after reading this book, you now have a better understanding of money (green), and how to make, save, and spend it. Remember, to discuss the things in this book with your parents or legal guardian's, so that they can also help you get on the right track with managing your money (green). Now, get ready and start applying these tips in your life that you just learned. It will help you as a kid, and will help ensure that you have a great future managing your money as an adult.

$ Glossary $

Account – is something that is assigned to you with a specific number that helps keep up with your money at the bank.

Allowance - money you get from your parents on a regular basis.

Bank - a place of business that keeps your money for you.

Balance - the amount of money you have in the bank.

Charity - organization that helps people in need with different things for free.

Chores – things you do around the house, like cleaning or making your bed.

Customers - people who pay you for services that you provide from your business.

Deposit - money that you put into your bank account.

Entrepreneurs - people who own their own business.

Financial Advisor - a person that helps you with how to save your money.

Green - money, dollars.

Interest - money that is paid to you for the use of your money by the bank.

Tithes & Offerings - money that you give to church to show honor to God.

Volunteer - when you help people for free.

Withdrawal - when you take your money out of the bank.

$ Helpful Websites $

www.upromise.com

www.treasurydirect.gov

www.themint.org

$ Write A List Of Your Own $
Business Ideas

_____

_____

_____

_____

_____

_____

_____

_____

_____

_____

_____

_____

_____

_____

_____

_____

_____

_____

_____

About the Authors

Tyrik Wynn is a teen author, and an aspiring journalist. He loves to volunteer and inspire teens. His goal for writing this book is to help enhance kid's knowledge about money, and the many ways to save, make it, and to be giving with it. He can be reached at tyrikwynn@yahoo.com.

T. Wynn is the mother of Tyrik Wynn, she is the co-author of this book. She currently has two other books under her belt entitled, "Make Sure Your Love Is Bigger Than Your Wedding!" and "Label Girl (Who Are You Wearing)". T. Wynn can be reached at twynnauthor@gmail.com or through her website, www.twynnauthor.com.

Tyrik Wynn & T. Wynn

Made in the USA
Columbia, SC
05 July 2022

62870358R00017